Go AHEAD & LIKE IT

JACQUELINE SUSKIN

i LIKE
IDylic SCENERY

Go Ahead & Like It

Jacqueline Suskin

Photographs: Shelby Duncan

Illustrations: Erielle Laniewski

Design: Laura Theobald
& Jacqueline Suskin

PASTE

TEN SPEED PRESS
Berkeley

I LIKE:

-Black ink
-The idea of a soulmate
-Walking through heaps of fallen leaves
-Snakes & lizards
-The first buds on a tree branch
-Giving compliments
-Collecting small things
-Naps
-Repetition
-The sound of a photo being taken
x-Glass bottle drinks
-Key lime pie
-Cotton clothing
-Making thank you cards
-Being on time
-Floral prints
-House slippers
-Knowing there is no such thing as the end
-Big bowls of icecream
-Early to be early to rise
-Craftsmanship
-Sitting in the same place daily to watch the sunset
-A single song played over and over
-Recycling wrapping paper
-First light

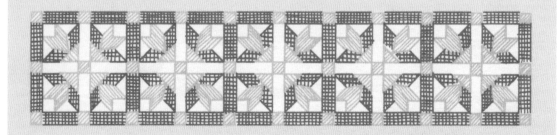

i like:

- watching the cat drink
- listening to the cat drink
- the movie Road House
- my own aroma
- clothes that i've worn since middle school
- calling people i haven't spoken with in years
- finding the colors that are unique in an otherwise monochromatic landscape.

I LIKE   MERIT BADGES
         CLOWN SHOES
         OLD PICTURES
         SKIPPING EVERY OTHER STAIR ON
             MY WAY UP
         CROOKED TEETH
         REMEMBERING
         LEMON IN MY WATER
         PECANS & PIE
         BLACK INK
         CROSSWORD PUZZLES THAT ARE JUST
             EASY ENOUGH
         HARRY DEAN STANTON (THE ACTOR)
         JAPANESE PEOPLE
         CHOO CHOO TRAINS
         CLASSIFIED ADS
         CARS WITH SPARE TIRES
         EATING CEREAL OUTSIDE
         ROOFTOPS
         MISMATCHED SOCKS
         VOYAGES
         DISORDERS

TO ОПО

WHO GAVE ME MY
FIRST
List of LIKES.

←

i LIKE:

- BUILDING FORTS
- WASHING MY FEET BEFORE GETTING INTO BED
- MIDDAY NAPS
- SINGING WHILE DRIVING/WALKING
- FLOSSING AFTER EATING A PEACH
- SCENTS THAT REMIND ME OF CERTAIN PLACES
- BREAD & BUTTER
- BEING AWARE OF MY POSTURE
- SHADOWS & LIGHT PATTERNS ON AN OTHERWISE BLANK WALL.

Go Ahead & Like It

Table of Contents

INTRODUCTION

An invitation to write your list of likes.

FOR YEARS I'VE BEEN WRITING LISTS OF THINGS THAT I LIKE. THIS IS MY PRACTICE OF SUSTAINED ELATION. MAKING THESE LISTS IS A CELEBRATION, A WAY TO NAME AND NOTE THE SIMPLICITIES OF LIFE BY CALLING THEM SACRED. THESE LISTS ARE MY APPRECIATION GUIDES— MY COLLECTED TOKENS THAT ENABLE ME TO BRING A QUALITY OF ATTENTION AND LOVE TO THE MINUTE AND REPETITIVE ASPECTS OF EXISTENCE. WITH SO MANY LISTS PILED UP AND SAVED, TUCKED INTO BOOKS AND STORED IN ENVELOPES, I DECIDED IT WAS ABOUT TIME TO OFFER UP SOME INSTRUCTION REGARDING THIS DEPENDABLE AND BENEFICIAL METHOD THAT HAS SERVED ME FOR SO LONG.

THERE ARE INFINITE AVENUES THAT I COULD TAKE TO PRESENT THIS PRACTICE, RANGING FROM PERSONAL STORIES THAT COINCIDE WITH CERTAIN LISTS, TO THE BROAD SPECTRUM OF WHAT IT MEANS TO LIKE THINGS IN THIS DAY AND AGE. INSTEAD OF TURNING TO CRITICAL ANALYSIS, INTIMATE HISTORY, OR WATERY PHILOSOPHY, I THOUGHT I'D JUST OFFER UP SOME HELPFUL WRITING HINTS AND A COMPENDIUM OF MY LISTS.

THE MOST INFLUENTIAL ASPECT OF LISTING MY LIKES IS THE INTROSPECTIVE ACT OF SIMPLY WRITING THE LIST ITSELF. MY HOPE IS TO PROVIDE EXAMPLES OF THIS MEDITATIVE EXERCISE THAT SO OFTEN RECONNECTS ME WITH THE MEANINGFUL DETAILS THAT FILL MY LIFE. TAKE IT AS A WRITING PROMPT, A MODEL FOR SELF-DISCOVERY, OR A FORM OF ACUTE OBSERVATION. HOWEVER ONE GOES ABOUT LISTING LIKES, IT IS AN INTERESTING PURSUIT AND AN OUTLET THAT PROVIDES MANY POSSIBILITIES...

I LIKE:
BEING UNDERWATER

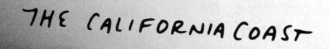

THE CALIFORNIA COAST

CHERRY-RED
EL CAMINOS

HOW TO WRITE A LIST of LIKES

At the top of the page write *i LIKE:*
Then, jot down the first thing that comes
to mind. If you can't think of anything
        just look around.
Find something in this very moment that
                delights you.

Perhaps it's just a color, or a photo
on the wall, or some other detail that
you can see.
            Try using all of your senses.

Can you smell something that really wows you?
Perhaps you can recall a scent that you enjoy.

Can you hear a sound that makes you excited?
Maybe it's a song on the radio
or the calming lull of the ceiling fan.

If your surroundings and your senses fail
to get your pen moving, try accessing
your memories.
Think back on yesterday, the week past,
or all the way back to your childhood.

Be as specific as possible.

Find the smallest details in order to create
a list that shows you how full your life is
with significant particulars.

FOR your FIRST FEW LISTING
ATTEMPTS, TRY TO WRITE
AT LEAST FIVE THINGS.

i LIKE:

- COMFORTABLE SHOES
- TOAST FOR BREAKFAST
- REMEMBERING MY DREAMS
- LONG CONVERSATIONS THAT ARE TO THE POINT
- STEADY DANCE PARTIES

WHEN & WHY: WRITE A LIST OF LIKES

My favorite time to write a list of likes is whenever I'm inspired to write one!

Usually, it's solely an act of celebration to mark a moment in which I'm particularly excited to be alive.

i LIKE WRITING OUTSIDE

But there are many reasons
I enjoy making these lists.
I've included some examples
of the ones I like the most:

- TEDIOUS SITUATIONS
- DURING SPELLS
      OF MELANCHOLY
- PASS NOTES & SEND MAIL
- A MEMORY EXERCISE
- PARLOR GAME,
      PARTY TRICK

TEDIOUS SITUATIONS

CERTAINLY, WE ALL GET STUCK IN TIRESOME AND FRUSTRATING CIRCUMSTANCES. WE HAVE TO WAIT IN A DOCTOR'S OFFICE FOR FAR TOO LONG, WE GET STUCK IN TRAFFIC, WE GET PUT ON HOLD, ETC.

LIFE IS FULL OF THESE FAMILIAR AND UNINSPIRING EPISODES. THIS IS A GREAT OPPORTUNITY TO JUST **GO AHEAD & LIKE IT.**

i LIKE DOGS WHO WAIT PATIENTLY FOR THEIR OWNERS.

PLEASE
GET OUT PAPER
& PEN OR JUST
MAKE A LIST
IN YOUR HEAD.

I enjoy this reason for assembling a list—
it's an amusing challenge. It's fun and invigorating
to ask myself to dig into a banal moment and pull out
a list of enjoyment where I might otherwise find nothing
but negativity. Typically, I discover that it feels much
better to emphasize the aspects of the moment that work
for me.

MY FAVORITE EXAMPLE
is THE TRAFFIC JAM

⟶

PASTE

Imagine
that you're on a
highway...

1.

YOU'RE ON YOUR
WAY HOME
FROM WORK—
YOU'RE TIRED
AND YOU'RE
STUCK IN TRAFFIC.

2.

PASTE

PASTE

WHAT CAN
YOU
≈ LIKE ≈
ABOUT THIS
MOMENT?

3.

Don't
think
    about it

too much.

4.

PASTE

PASTE

Simply
    look
        around...

5.

i LIKE: THE VINES GROWING
OVER THE EMBANKMENTS, THE
FANTASTIC TURQUOISE PAINT
JOB ON THE CAR IN FRONT
OF ME, THE THOUSANDS
OF CHERRY BLOSSOMS
IN THE FIELD I'M PASSING,
THE SONG THAT'S ON THE
RADIO, THE SMOOTHNESS
OF MY SOCKS INSIDE
MY SHOES... 6.

PASTE

Bellyaching about trivial woes doesn't help me realize release. No matter how much I moan, I'm still going to have to trudge through some uninteresting occasions. So I ask myself, wouldn't it be wiser to find a more enjoyable focus and appreciate the beauty of the giant oak tree on the right, or visualize the healthy eggplants waiting to be picked in the garden? Even at its most monotonous, isn't life actually worth celebrating?

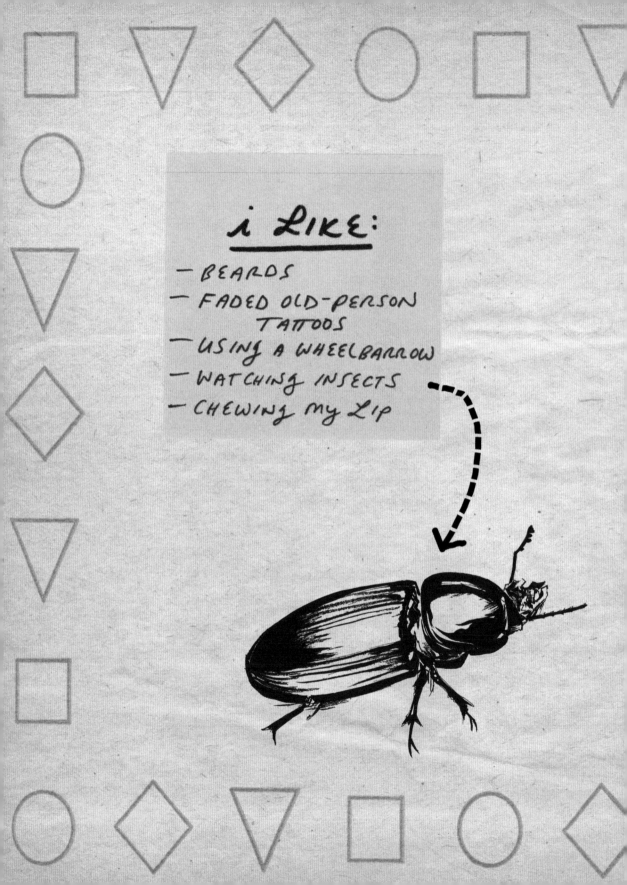

i LIKE:

- Saying yes
- BREATHING COOL AIR WHILE i SLEEP
- USING A WIDE-TOOTH COMB
- BLACK INK
- SPITTING CHERRY PITS
- TAPIOCA PUDDING
- CURSIVE
- MAKING/SENDING THANK YOU CARDS
- THE IDEA OF A SOULMATE
- SPENDING THE ENTIRE DAY ALONE.
- WAVING AT FOLKS AS i PASS BY
- BRUSHING SAND OUT OF THE BED
- LUMBER RACKS ON PICK-UP TRUCKS
- WAITING WHILE THE TEA STEEPS.
- CELEBRATING THE NEW + THE FULL MOON
- SKYLIGHTS — SWEEPING THE FLOOR
- SLEEPING IN A TREEHOUSE
- CANDIED GINGER — BUILDING A FIRE
- THE WORD: SUPPER. — NEWSPRINT
- SLICED TOMATOES WITH SALT + PEPPER
- OLD SHEETS

DURING SPELLS OF MELANCHOLY

SOMETIMES WHEN SADNESS SETTLES IN
IT'S HELPFUL TO MAKE A LIST.
I'VE NEVER HAD A LIST OF LIKES PULL ME
OUT OF DEPRESSION OR MIRACULOUSLY ZING ME
INTO PERFECT HAPPINESS. I'VE NEVER ATTEMPTED
TO USE THIS LISTING METHOD DURING MOMENTS
OF TRAGEDY. YET, I DO FIND COMFORT
AND SUITABLE CONSOLATION IN MAKING A LIST
WHEN I'M GLUM.

IF ANYTHING, LOOKING AROUND
WITH A DIFFERENT PERSPECTIVE
OR SUMMONING BACK SENSATIONS
OF GLADNESS IS A HEALTHY CHANGE—
EVEN IF THE DIFFERENCE ONLY
LASTS FOR AS LONG AS IT
TAKES TO MAKE THE
LIST.

i LIKE BIRDS
IN FLIGHT

i LIKE EATING A FEAST AFTER A NEAR-DEATH EXPERIENCE

I've often asked myself to practice
this form of self-advocacy
when I'm feeling low.

The results have been a shrug of the shoulders
and the thought:

i GUESS THINGS AREN'T THAT BAD...

Other times, I've forced myself to make a list
and it's been ineffective.

When I focus on the details I like, I usually
end up feeling better and appreciating some
greatness that I overlooked. Noting the available
specifics normally brings me into closer connection
with the world around me. Ideally, when we take time
to open ourselves up to the things we like, we will
be more likely to appreciate the significance
of the things that surround us.

i LIKE: DRIVING ALONE.

PASS NOTES & SEND MAIL

i ENJOY sending LISTS of LIKES ALONG WITH LETTERS TO FRIENDS AND LOVERS.

- o DEAR EARL,
- o i LIKE: CLING PEACHES,
- o WATCHING BIRDS TAKE
- o DIRT BATHS, BOOK STORES,
- o LAKE SWIMMING, NAPS,
- o THE BANJO, AND STORMS.
- o ♡

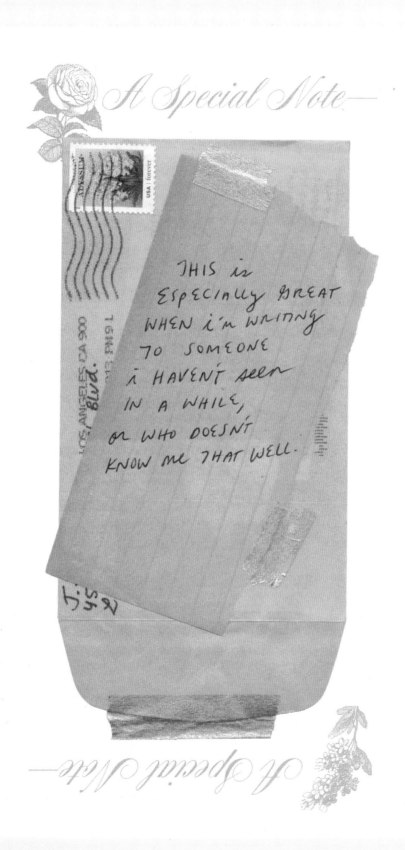

THIS is
ESPECIALLY GREAT
WHEN i'm WRITING
TO SOMEONE
i HAVEN'T seen
IN A WHILE,
oR WHO DOESN'T
KNOW me THAT WELL.

i FIND THAT A LIST OF LIKES
is A TERRIFIC INTRODUCTION.
By offering up THE Day-To-Day
SPECIFICS THAT ARE IMPORTANT
TO ME, i SHOW WHAT i CARE
ABOUT AND NOTICE in THE WORLD.

i LIKE
CORMORANTS

i LIKE
SEA
STACKS

i LIKE:

BULL KELP

GREY HAIR

i LIKE:

- TO PET THE MUZZLE
        OF A HORSE.
- LIVING ROOM DANCE PARTIES.
- BIG, CROOKED, STRANGE TEETH.
- NAKED RIVER SWIMMING.
- GRASS GROWING ON ROOFTOPS.
- BRICK SIDEWALKS & STREETS.
- CLEAN TEETH.
- FINDING LITTLE TREASURES
        ON THE GROUND.
- HAIRCUTS ON THE PORCH.
- OLD PAPER.
- HIGH CEILINGS.

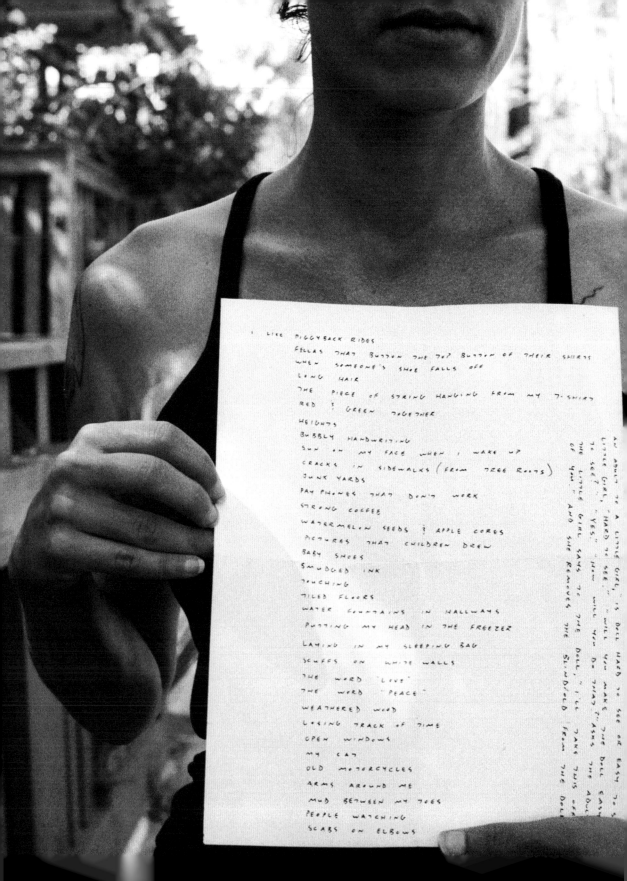

I LIKE PIGGYBACK RIDES
FELLAS THAT BUTTON THE TOP BUTTON OF THEIR SHIRTS
WHEN SOMEONE'S SHOE FALLS OFF
LONG HAIR
THE PIECE OF STRING HANGING FROM MY T-SHIRT
RED & GREEN TOGETHER
HEIGHTS
BUBBLY HANDWRITING
SUN ON MY FACE WHEN I WAKE UP
CRACKS IN SIDEWALKS (FROM TREE ROOTS)
JUNK YARDS
PAY PHONES THAT DON'T WORK
STRONG COFFEE
WATERMELON SEEDS & APPLE CORES
PICTURES THAT CHILDREN DREW
BABY SHOES
SMUDGED INK
TOUCHING
TILED FLOORS
WATER FOUNTAINS IN HALLWAYS
PUTTING MY HEAD IN THE FREEZER
LAYING IN MY SLEEPING BAG
SCUFFS ON WHITE WALLS
THE WORD "LOVE"
THE WORD "PEACE"
WEATHERED WOOD
LOSING TRACK OF TIME
OPEN WINDOWS
MY CAT
OLD MOTORCYCLES
ARMS AROUND ME
MUD BETWEEN MY TOES
PEOPLE WATCHING
SCABS ON ELBOWS

AN ADULT IS A LITTLE GIRL, IS DOLL HARD TO SEE OR EASY TO SEE?
LITTLE GIRL, "HARD TO SEE." "I WILL HELP YOU MAKE THE DOLL EASY
TO SEE." "YES." "HOW WILL YOU DO THAT?" ASKS THE ADULT.
THE LITTLE GIRL SAYS TO THE DOLL, "I'LL TAKE THIS OFF
OF YOU." AND SHE REMOVES THE BLINDFOLD FROM THE DOLL

THIS is HOW i FIRST CAME TO DISCOVER THE JOY IN WRITING LISTS of LIKES: A FRIEND HANDED ME A NOTE IN THE FIRST WEEK of OUR RELATIONSHIP THAT CONSISTED of A SINGLE PAGE of THINGS THAT HE LIKED. THIS SIMPLE GIFT ALLOWED ME TO SEE SOME of THE INTRICACY of HIS DAILY EXPERIENCES AND TO KNOW HIM IN AN IMMEDIATE AND INTIMATE WAY. FROM THAT MOMENT, i BECAME DEDICATED TO CRAFTING LISTS of MY OWN AND HAVE SINCE GIVEN MANY AWAY AS TOKENS of MY AFFECTION.

i LIKE:

LIMOGES DEMITASSE AND SAUCER
IN WHITE AND GOLD
ONLY $2.00 (COMPARABLE VALUE UP TO $6)

Genuine Limoges demitasse and saucer, pure white, with simp
gold design fired over with the transparent glaze that protec
this treasure for generations. Translucent, almost eggshell-thi
Magnificent for dinner or decor. Mailed from France. Allow
weeks for delivery.

#58. USE ORDER FORM IN BACK OF BOOK

27

SELEC
FROM MA
ONLY 75¢ (COMPARA

Select-A-Notes are 20 cheery
folded, which can be transfor
ing on the proper caption, u
white envelopes, 40 caption
green, pale violet, tastefully e
from U.S. Allow 3 to 5 weeks

#24. USE ORDER F

HOT TEA
IN THE MORNING

QUALITY

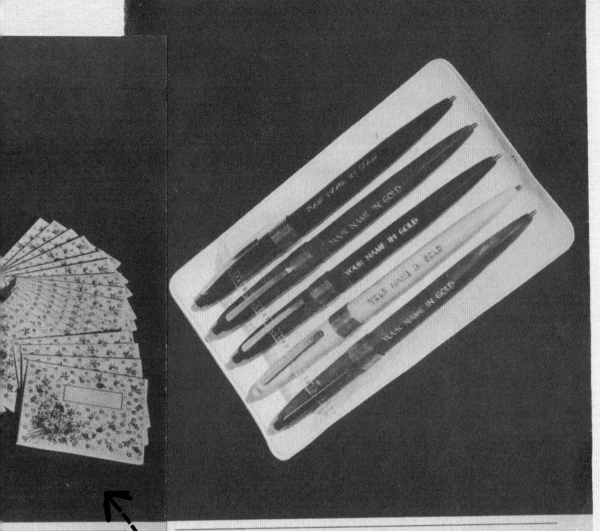

5 PERSONALIZED BALLPOINT PENS
MADE IN NEW YORK
5 ONLY 75¢ (COMPARABLE VALUE UP TO $1.50)

For the student, housewife, or businessman who is always losing pens, here is the perfect answer: five! Each has a different color ink: red, blue, green, black, gold. Each has your first and last name in bronze. Mailed from U.S. Allow 3 to 5 weeks.

#23. USE ORDER FORM IN BACK OF BOOK

STATIONARY

BALL POINT
PENS

A MEMORY EXERCISE

REVIEW YOUR PAST & ALL ITS BOUNTY!

NO MATTER HOW I'M FEELING, IT'S ALWAYS A GREAT EVENT WHEN I REVIEW MY LISTS. THEY CAN SERVE AS A COMPREHENSIVE TIMELINE, DESCRIBING THE ORNATE BOUNTY I'VE COLLECTED OVER THE years AND AS A REMINDER OF AN UNENDING SOURCE OF INTRIGUE.

i LIKE FOXGLOVES

AND PEAR BLOSSOMS

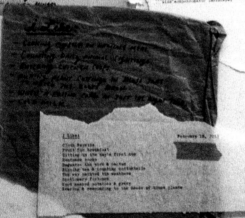

Each will display evidence about the past and refresh
the present with elements that moved you once and will
perhaps move you again as you reread.

i LIKE
PLANT TUNNELS

One of my favorite things to do is follow a line of memories.
It starts with a single recollection, an event or image
from the past, that can unravel and allow me to
travel backwards to view my history.

TRY STARTING
WITH A CHILDHOOD
MEMORY

We complete crossword puzzles, fiddle with number problems and take supplements to enhance our powers of remembrance.

We look at old photo albums and reread our journals to refresh our idea of what's happened in our lives.

Lists of Likes can provide a similar overview.

While creating the list, you can choose to focus on your memories as opposed to the present moment. Try and conjure up specifics that have moved you in the past and follow the lead of these likeable instances.

I've come up with details and images that I'd forgotten, bits of life from times I'd failed to keep in mind.

Restoring one set of memories can help reveal countless others. By writing some of these down as a list of likes, we supply ourselves with a bank that can be revisited when a spark of yesterday is needed.

i LIKE SURPRISE PARTIES

PARLOR GAME, PARTY TRICK

DURING THE PROCESS OF WRITING THIS BOOK,
i WAS AT A SMALL PARTY WHERE i ONLY KNEW
ONE PERSON. i WAS ENJOYING THE COMPANY
AND i FELT INSPIRED TO ASK THE GROUP
IF THEY WOULD BE INTERESTED IN MAKING LISTS of LIKES.

i THOUGHT IT WOULD BE A FUN WAY FOR ALL of US
TO INTERACT AND GET AQUAINTED. Surprisingly,
EVERYONE WAS EXCITED TO TRY MY GAME. WE SAT
DOWN IN A CIRCLE, i PASSED OUT PENS AND PAPER,
AND WE TOOK ABOUT TEN MINUTES TO WRITE FIVE
THINGS THAT EACH of US LIKED.

DATE	QUANTITY	ITEM No. AND NAME	COST

When we finished, we passed the lists around so that folks could read them anonymously. Eventually, we started to read xxx aloud, and people were excited to claim their own. A few had even written some of the same likes.

We were able to bond over our lists and it seemed to be a x fun experience for the entire group.

In a single evening we discovered yet another satisfying way to engage with writing lists!

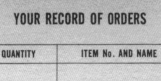

i LIKE:

OTHER PEOPLE'S LISTS & LIKES

i like:

warmth
coolness
crackers
wood
brown

i LIKE
BROWN & BLACK
Together

I Like Country Music
I Like Whiskey
I Like Dancing
I Like Dirt roads
I Like weed
I Like country girls
I Like city girls
I Like fishing
I Like hunting
I Like riding my bike
I Like my good friends
I Like my family
I Like my truck
I Like that I do and don't give
a fuck
I Like love
I Like hats
I Like Bibs
I Like Beer

Dig DEEPER & ASK WHY

ANOTHER WAY THAT i INTERACT WITH MY LISTS is BY GOING BACK OVER THEM AND ASKING MYSELF **WHY** i LIKE THE THINGS THAT i WROTE DOWN. THIS CAN BE A SIMPLE <u>WRITING EXERCISE</u>, A PROMPT THAT GETS IDEAS FLOWING, OR AN AVENUE of DEEPER <u>SELF-DISCOVERY</u>.

We're living in a surge of likeability.

With the click of a button we like one another's lives. But what's really happening on the other end of the click? Do we know <u>why</u> we like the things that we like? Are we able to reflect on them later and go beyond the images of our friend's lifestyles to understand the meaning behind our likes?

Knowing <u>why</u> these details affect us the way they do isn't always possible. Sometimes, we just like something. A flower simply smells good and we enjoy it, not because it reminds us of our grandmother or living in Spain, but just because it's pleasing. Other times are more specific: we might admire a garden fence because it's exactly the same as the one surrounding our family home.

i LIKE
TOOTHY SMILES

Printed in U.S.A.

NO MATTER THE REASONS
BEHIND THE LISTS,
THEY HAVE THE POWER
TO PROVIDE US WITH
REMINDERS OF WHAT
DELIGHTS US. BY ASKING
WHY, WE CAN DISCOVER
THE RICHNESS IN THE
ASPECTS OF LIFE THAT
CAPTURE OUR
ATTENTION.

AT TIMES I REVEL
IN TAKING A FEW
EXAMPLES from
MY LISTS TO USE
AS WRITING PROMPTS.

I ASK MYSELF TO ANSWER
THE QUESTION:

WHY DO I LIKE THIS?

I DON'T FEEL THE NEED TO DO
THIS WITH EVERY DETAIL ON
A LIST, BUT A FEW WILL
STAND OUT AND INSPIRE
ME TO LOOK CLOSER.

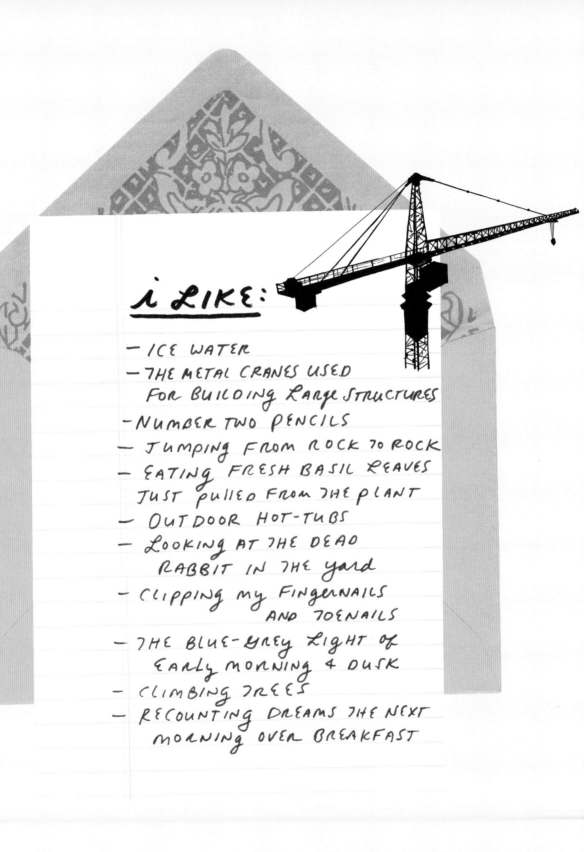

i LIKE:

- ICE WATER
- THE METAL CRANES USED FOR BUILDING LARGE STRUCTURES
- NUMBER TWO PENCILS
- JUMPING FROM ROCK TO ROCK
- EATING FRESH BASIL LEAVES JUST PULLED FROM THE PLANT
- OUTDOOR HOT-TUBS
- LOOKING AT THE DEAD RABBIT IN THE yard
- CLIPPING MY FINGERNAILS AND TOENAILS
- THE BLUE-GREY LIGHT OF EARLY MORNING & DUSK
- CLIMBING TREES
- RECOUNTING DREAMS THE NEXT MORNING OVER BREAKFAST

i LIKE
     LOOKING
AT THE DEAD RABBIT
     IN THE YARD

This exercise of asking and answering usually feels as satisfying
as opening up a surprise package. *HERE ARE SOME EXAMPLES:*

Why do I like eating fresh basil leaves just pulled from the plant?

Because they hold the most sun.
Because the taste reminds me of being eight years old and picking
from my mother's plants in the green house. What a treat to taste
her creation! How honored I was when she would allow me to enter
her warm glasshouse and eat from her prized plants. She'd collect
the leaves and blend them with her tomatoes to make the sweetest
sauce.

Why do I like looking at the dead rabbit in the yard?

Because it's finally still enough for me to study.
I can touch its soft fur, its perfect ears, and gather xxxxndxxx
an understanding of its prior ability. I can kneel low and look
into its eyes, curl its lip to appreciate small teeth, pink gums,
and memorize the specifics of such specialized paws that are uxx
made for motion. I can know it in a way that only death or
domestication provides. This wild one, struck by a car, would
never have allowed me such comprehensive investigation while
breathing. Its sad passing permits me to learn its features
and xx sanctify its body as a collection of details that help
me see its living cousins with completeness never before realizd
                                                     realized.

Why do I like number two pencils?

Because they seem appropriate for every moment.
Worth carrying, keeping sharp and ready for words.
Because of their sound on the page, their just-so thickness,
and the scent of their shavings. Because graphite is such a
pleasing name and a naturally occuring mineral. Because of the
standard look, the reliable yellow painted body, the kindly
included eraser. Best used for my handwriting on newsprint.
Used to show the size of the infinitesimal bee hummingbird
that can rest with ease on the eraser and so show off its minute
stature. Scribing my poems for years, the curve of cursive, the
subtleness of grey as opposed to the boldness of ink. Good to hold
between teeth and make my mark with molars. Good behind the ear,
spotted on the ground from the bus window, familiar and bright.

i LIKE:

ADORNING
my
VEHICLE

THE MANY
USES OF
TAPE

i LIKE:

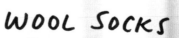
WOOL SOCKS

I Like: February 18, 2013

Cloth Napkins
Fruit for breakfast
Sitting in the day's first sun
Handmade books
Saguaro- the word & cactus
Sipping tea & counting cottontails
The way painted tin weathers
Dictionary fortunes
Good mashed potatoes & gravy
Hearing & responding to the needs of house plants

RAT-TAILS

CONCLUSION

WHEN WE LIST THE THINGS THAT WE LIKE, ON OUR HIGHWAY DRIVE, ON OUR WALK TO THE STORE, IN ANY MOMENT, WE ARE POLISHING OUR UNDERSTANDING OF HOW LIFE CONTINUES TO CAPTIVATE US.

LET YOUR LISTS BE REMINDERS OF ENCHANTMENT, IMPLEMENTS OF REVERIE, LOVING MISSIVES, OR HEALING ADVISORS.

HOWEVER THE PROCESS WORKS BEST FOR YOU, JUST

GO AHEAD & LIKE IT.

i LIKE:

- FRESH GRAPES RIGHT OFF
  THE VINE
- SHOWING UP SOMEWHERE NEW
  IN THE DARK
- PIE (ESPECIALLY RHUBARB)
- BRUISES
- DOGS WAITING PATIENTLY
  FOR THEIR OWNERS
- LIGHTING A CANDLE WITH
  ANOTHER CANDLE
- OLD SUITCASES
- CURING SPECIFIC CRAVINGS
- COOKING BIG MEALS
- READING ALOUD
- SEEING THE PERSON WHO
  GAVE ME THE HAND-ME-DOWN
  THAT i'm WEARING
- RECOGNIZING FAMILIAR PLANTS

i LiKe iT wHEN TREE RooTs

DISRUPT THE SIDEWALK

i LIKE: you
ACKNOWLEDGEMENTS

Laura Theobald, design master and gracious host, I could not have done this without you.

Shelby Duncan, for beautiful photographs and undying belief.

Erielle Laniewski, for beautiful illustrations and unconditional friendship.

My kind and patient editors: Meredith Clark, Ginny Grimsley, Sarah Sky, Sacha Marini, Megan May, Liz Kimbrough, Matthew Phipps, Robert Pellicer, and especially John Michaels.

Douglas Ferguson, Oliver Newell, and Tyler Kohlhoff for helping me form ideas beyond the lists. Maira Kalman for infinite inspiration. Matthew Stadler for "my practice of sustained elation" and other perfect translations. George Augusto, for welcoming me into the inspiring clan of Dilettante. Michael Shifflett, for believing in my career and helping me craft it. Andrew Poyner for love and support. Thomas Dammann for lending me a room and a desk. Amber Maywald for sharing the gulch. Omar Wilson for sharing the desert. Tops, Jenny O, Saul Simon MacWilliams, Taylor Jabe Feltner, Noah Gershman, Rachel Zingoni, Neal Ewald, Lindsey Byers, Emily Alden Foster, Adam Prince, and of course Zachary Houston.

To all of you who sent me your lists of likes, you helped this project grow.

Thank you.

WRITE YOUR OWN
LIST OF LIKES

- 1.

- 2.

- 3.

- 4.

- 5.

ABOUT THE AUTHOR

Jacqueline Suskin operates a performance poetry piece informally referred to as "Poem Store"—a project that consists of exchanging on-demand poetry on any subject composed on a manual typewriter in exchange for a donation. Her first book of poetry is *The Collected* (Publication Studio, 2010). She lives in Los Angeles, California.

Published in the United States by Ten Speed Press, an imprint of the Crown Publishing
Group, a division of Random House LLC, a Penguin Random House Company, New York.
www.crownpublishing.com
www.tenspeed.com

Ten Speed Press and the Ten Speed Press colophon are registered trademarks of
Random House LLC.

Originally published in the United States by Dilettante,
Los Angeles, California, in 2014.
PAPER

Library of Congress Cataloging-in-Publication Data

Suskin, Jacqueline.
Go ahead and like it / Jacqueline Suskin; photographs, Shelby Duncan; illustrations, Erielle
Laniewski. — First Ten Speed Press edition.
    pages cm
  "Originally published in the United States by Dilettante Paper, Los Angeles, in 2014."
  Summary: "An artistic self-help book that prompts and inspires readers to write lists of
things they like—a simple yet profound way to collect and remember the good in daily
life"—Provided by publisher.
1. Contentment—Miscellanea. 2. Likes and dislikes—Miscellanea. 3. Gratitude—
Miscellanea. 4. Self-realization—Miscellanea. I. Title.
  BJ1533.C7.S87 2015
  158.1—dc23
                          2014045313

Hardcover ISBN: 978-1-60774-877-9
eBook ISBN: 978-1-60774-878-6

Printed in China

Design by Laura Theobald & Jacqueline Suskin

10 9 8 7 6 5 4 3 2 1

First Ten Speed Press Edition